AT THE
POST OFFICE

By LILLIAN COLONIUS and GLENN W. SCHROEDER

MELMONT PUBLISHERS, INC., Chicago

ACKNOWLEDGMENT

The authors wish to thank Mr. Larry Anderson of the Public Relations Department of the Los Angeles Post Office for his cooperation in the preparation of this book.

TABLE OF CONTENTS

THE MAIL CARRIER

One morning Mary saw the mail carrier coming to her home. She ran out to get the mail. The carrier was driving a three wheeled car called a "mailster."

Mary said, "I am surprised to see that you are not using the push cart to deliver our mail."

The mail carrier said, "The 'mailster' is faster and better for me to use than the push cart. I can carry all of the mail for my route in the 'mailster.' Some of the carriers use the push carts. It is a better way to deliver mail to office buildings and stores downtown."

Mary went into her house and told her mother about the carrier and the "mailster."

Mary's mother, Mrs. Allen, said, "I have a package to mail tomorrow. If you want to know more about the mail and the post office, you may come with me."

THE POST OFFICE LOBBY

The next day, Mrs. Allen told Mary that she was ready to go to the post office. Mary's brother, Roger, went with them. He wanted to learn more about the mail, too.

Mrs. Allen and the children looked at the many windows in the post office lobby. There was a window where people bought stamps. There was a window where people mailed packages.

There was a window for general delivery mail. General delivery mail has no street address on it. The mail has the words "General Delivery" on it. People who are in town for a short time call for their mail at this window.

Mary said, "What are those rows of locked boxes with numerals on them?"

Mrs. Allen told Mary that the post office rents post-office boxes. Some people and businesses like to get their mail without waiting for it to be delivered.

MAILING A PACKAGE

Roger carried the package that his mother wanted to mail. The clerk at the window weighed the package on the scales. She used the postage meter to make the stamp needed to mail the package.

The clerk smiled and said, "Your package is addressed as it should be. Your return address is on it. It is wrapped so that it will not break open. I wish all packages were wrapped and addressed as well as this one."

The clerk put the package with many other packages. Mary and Roger tried to see what she was doing. The clerk said, "These packages will be sorted for different cities. They will be put into large bags that we call pouches. Some of the pouches will be taken to the station and put onto trains. Some of the pouches will be taken to the airport to go by plane."

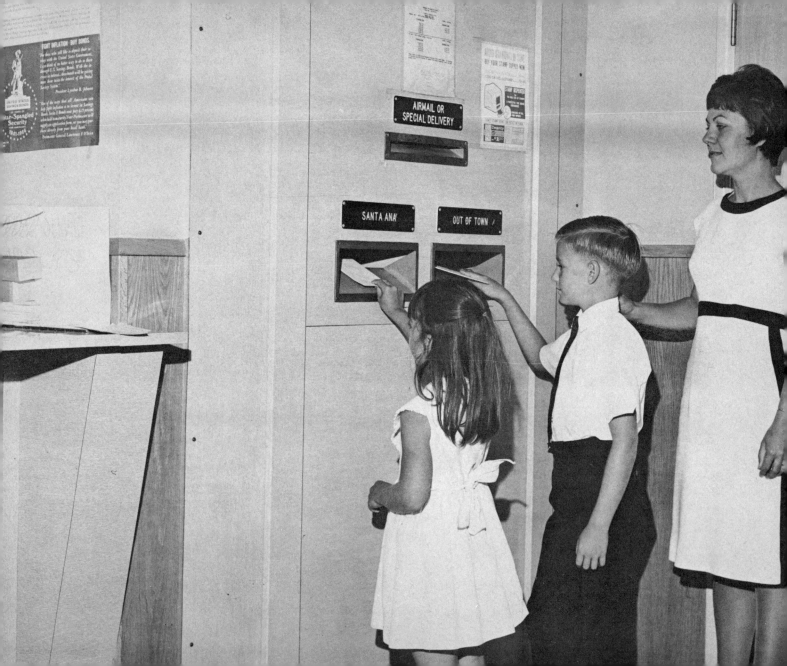

MAILING LETTERS

Mary and Roger brought letters to mail. They needed stamps. They bought stamps at the stamp window.

The children and their mother went over to the mailing slots. They read what was written over each slot. Mary said, "My letter is going to someone in our city. I shall drop it into the slot for local mail."

Roger said, "My letter is going to New York. I shall drop it into the slot for letters that go out-of-town. Look, there is a slot for both air mail and special delivery letters."

Mary said, "I wonder where the letters go after they are put into the mailing slots?"

THE FACING TABLE

Mrs. Allen asked if the children might see how the mail went through the post office. Mr. Sands was their guide. He took them back to a facing table.

Mr. Sands said, "Roger, your letter to New York will come back to the facing table. It has two slots. One is for long envelopes. One is for short envelopes.

"As the workers sort the envelopes, they face them. This means the envelopes are turned so that the stamps are in the lower left hand corner.

"Air mail, special delivery, and odd-sized letters are not put into the slots. They are put in boxes above the table. They are canceled separately. Some post offices are using facing machines that help to speed up the mail."

The Facing Table

THE CANCELING MACHINE

The letters were moved from the facing table to the canceling machine. A worker put the letters through the machine. The canceling machine printed lines across each stamp to cancel it. Now the stamp could not be used again.

The canceling machine stamped the name of the city on each stamp. It stamped the name of the state. It stamped the date. It stamped A.M. for before noon or P.M. for afternoon. Hundreds of letters go through a canceling machine in a minute.

Mary said, "The next time I see a postmark on a letter I'll know how it got there."

After the children looked at the canceling machine, their guide took them to the sorting case.

SORTING THE MAIL

The children saw a clerk working at a sorting case. In front of him were many rows of little boxes. The clerk looked at the address on each letter. He put the letters into the boxes.

The clerk stopped working long enough to say, "I am sorting the local mail. This is called primary sorting. Letters going to the same place are put together for the first time. The mail will go to the post-office stations in our city. The mail carriers will sort the mail for their routes."

Mr. Sands said, "We can see clerks sorting the mail for other cities and states. It will be the primary sorting for that mail, too. Then later, the mail is sorted at another case. The letters going to the same large cities are put together. This is the secondary sorting of the mail."

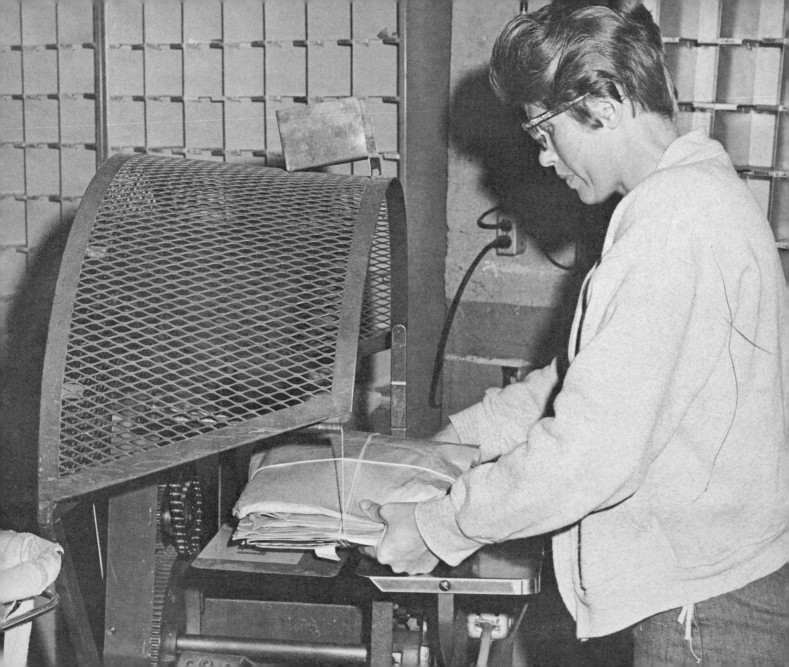

THE ZIP CODE

The guide told the children that one of the biggest changes in the delivery of mail was the use of the Zip Code. He said, "It is using a code in numerals in addressing mail. The post office has sent a card to your home with your Zip Code numerals on it. It tells you how to use the Zip Code on your mail.

"There are machines to help speed the mail addressed with the Zip Code along. It will save time and money for the post office.

"It is important that the Zip Code is used on all the mail you send. You should put your Zip Code on your return address, too."

Mary and Roger watched a worker using a tying machine. The bundles of out-of-town mail were tied with string by the machine.

FILLING THE MAIL POUCHES

A worker tossed the out-of-town mail into pouches that were on racks. Roger saw the names of the cities or states and the Zip Code on the racks. The worker had learned where to put the mail. He worked very fast because he had done it so often.

Mr. Sands took a mail pouch and showed the children how it was closed and locked. He said, "Only a post office worker with a key can unlock the pouch. Each pouch is marked with the place where it is being sent and how it is to go there."

The locked pouches were loaded onto a hand truck. The hand truck was pushed out to the loading platform.

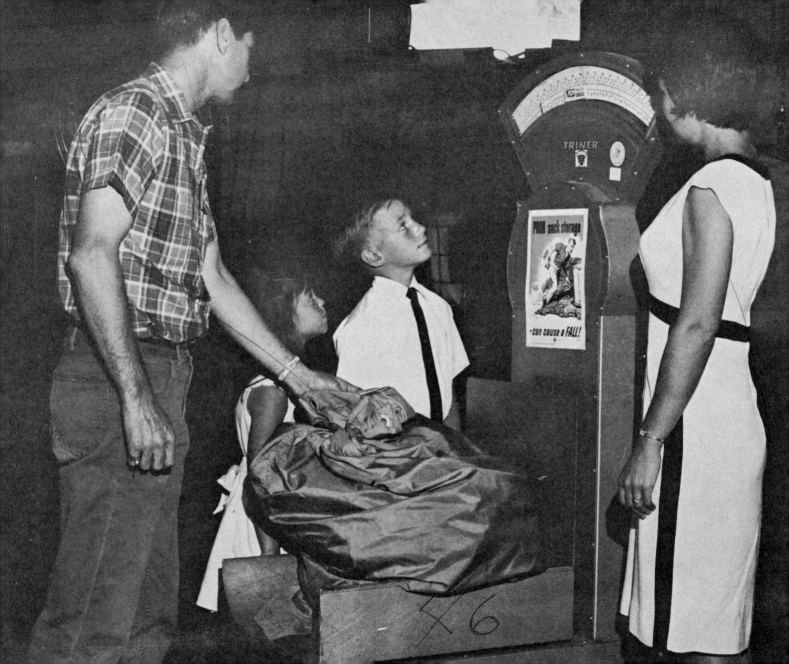

AIR MAIL POUCHES

Roger and Mary saw a big scale near some orange colored pouches. A worker weighed a pouch. He saw the children watching him. He said, "The orange colored pouches are for air mail. A pouch of air mail must not weigh more than fifty pounds. It must not be too heavy for a person to lift into an airplane."

The worker wrote the weight of each pouch of air mail on a card. He put a card on each pouch. He loaded the pouches onto a hand truck.

Mr. Sands said, "Let's go out to the loading platform."

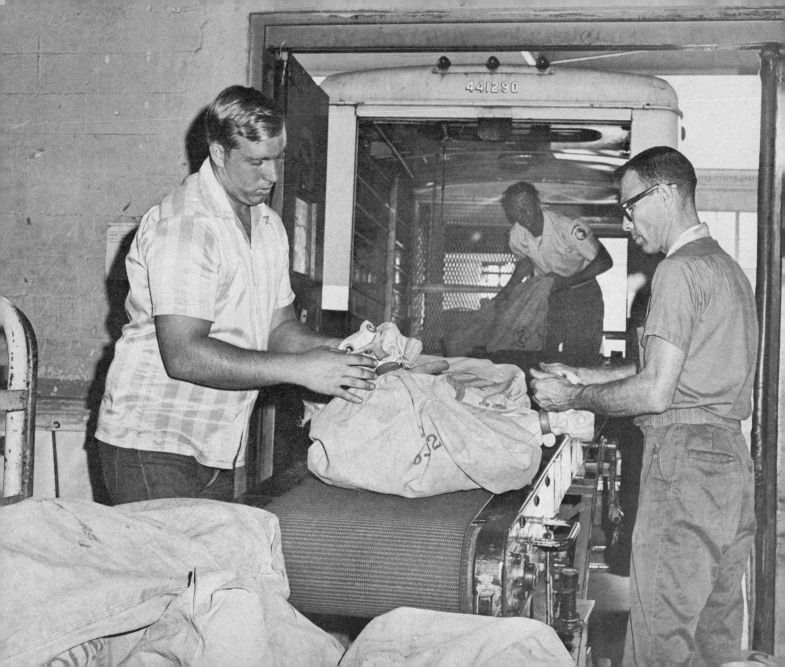

THE LOADING PLATFORM

Mrs. Allen and the children went out to the loading platform. A mail truck drove up. The driver opened the back doors of the truck.

Two workers loaded the pouches of mail onto a moving belt. They looked at the tags on the pouches to be sure that the pouches were going into the right truck. The mail moved up into the truck.

Roger asked, "Where will the driver take the mail?"

Mr. Sands answered, "He will take the mail to the railroad stations. Other trucks will take the air mail to the airport."

The children thanked Mr. Sands for showing them around the post office.

Mary's mother said, "How much we have learned about the mail this morning. Now we must go home. Let's go to the airport tomorrow to find out more about air mail."

MAIL COLLECTION

The next day Mary, Roger and Mrs. Allen were ready to go to the airport. Mary said, "I wrote a letter to Mr. Sands and thanked him for our trip through the post office yesterday. Where shall I mail it?"

Roger said, "You could take it to the collection box down on the corner of our street. Or, you could give it to the mail carrier here at home. He can take it back to the post office for you."

Mrs. Allen said, "I know another way to mail a letter. Bring the letter with you. We can drive up to a curb-side collection box on our way to the airport. You don't need to get out of the car. You just reach out of the car window and drop the letter into the box."

Mary said, "I think your way will be fun."

Curb-side Collection Box

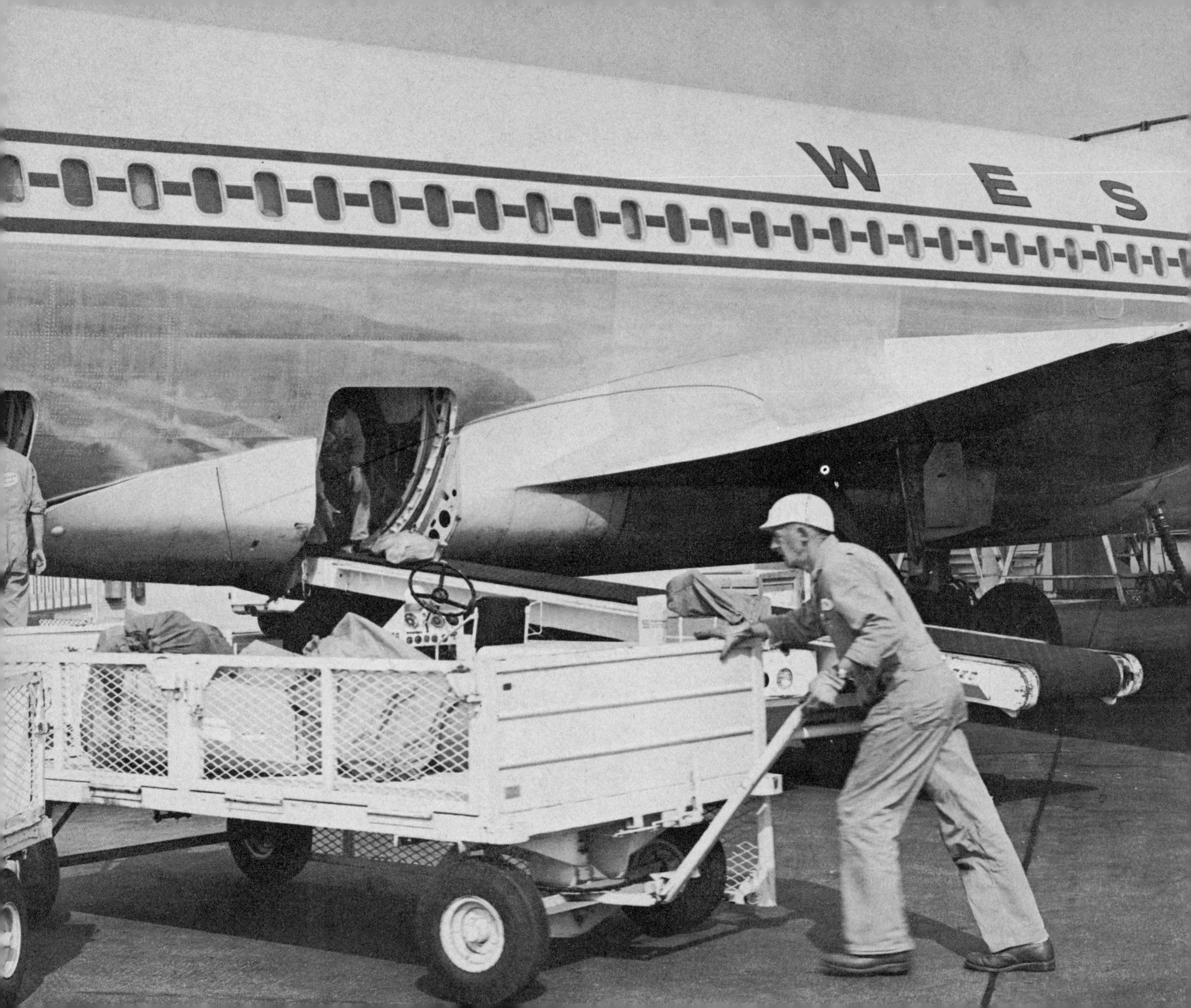
W E S

THE AIRPORT POST OFFICE

Mary and Roger went with their mother to a large airport. She said, "There is a post office at many of the large airports. Mail is brought to the airport from other post offices. Mail pouches are sorted in the airport post office. Then the pouches are loaded into carts and pulled out to the airplanes."

Roger said, "Look at the cart of mail that the men are unloading."

Mrs. Allen said, "We can watch the pouches of air mail move on a belt up to the airplane. A worker puts the mail into the cargo space of the airplane."

Roger said, "I am so glad that we could come to the airport. I want to see the jet take off with the mail."

Loading Mail into a Plane

THE AUTOMATED POST OFFICE

On the way home from the airport, Mary said, "We just went by a different kind of post office. May we go back and look at it?"

Mrs. Allen said, "Yes, let's drive in by the post office. I read about the automated post offices in the newspaper. They can be in shopping centers. We can get out of the car and look at the machines."

"Here is a machine that can make change for one dollar bills and coins. You can buy stamps, stamped envelopes, and postcards in the other machines," said Roger.

Mary said, "You can weigh a package on the scales and find out how much postage is needed to mail it."

Mrs. Allen told the children that there was a phone line to the nearest post office to answer questions.

Mary said, "Thank you, Mother, for helping us to learn more about the mail."

Lillian Colonius is a graduate of Occidental College in Los Angeles, California. She has had considerable experience teaching first, second, and third grade children. At present she is a second grade teacher in the Santa Ana, California, public schools.

Although Glenn Schroeder is a printer by trade, he has also been a free lance photographer for a number of years.

Mrs. Colonius and Mr. Schroeder prepared this book with the thought in mind that it might fill a need for more supplementary social studies material in the classroom. The publishers hope that the book will also prove stimulating leisure reading for children.